The Layers Between

Celia Claase

In **The Layers Between**, natural phenomena such as Matter, Water and Space are given their own voices; Philosophical concepts like Entropy, Consciousness and Information are allowed to speak for themselves; "Yin and Yan" and the biblical figure "Eve" narrate their own stories. By employing recognized scientific findings to introduce a fresh – some may call a fantastical – hypothesis, the writer defamiliarises the origins of our universe, the workings of our bodies, of our minds and life itself. In this first section of the book she explains how "everything" and "nothing" are the opposite poles of one energy-frequency with a myriad scales of information layered between. She knows very well that this is a theory of mind yet to be verified; nevertheless bravely challenges existing "Theories of Everything".

The second section in the book consists of poems that draw the reader back into everyday life and its many speculative questions, by taking a closer look at the transient state of nature under the influence of time; how humans nestle into the spaces that matter provides; our attraction to and curiosity about the surreal and the spiritual; the consciousness within all sensory experiences; our craving for connective relationships and how everything that has been mentioned is nothing but recycled works of art.

Celia Claase grew up and studied in South Africa where she taught young minds for many years. In 2008, her family relocated to Hong Kong where she has been working as an ESL teacher ever since. In her free time she writes and works on her latest series of oil paintings. Her art has been exhibited and sold in South Africa as well as Hong Kong. As a member of the Women in Publishing Society Hong Kong, she acts as coordinator of their annual short story competition for young writers. *Sarie*, a South African magazine, featured her memoirs for a period of several months and she has had poetry published in literary journals such as *Imprint* and *Writers Abroad*. Winner of a LitNet flash fiction prize, she also received an award from the Hong Kong Schools Drama Festival for writing an outstanding stage script. Celia, like the poet R.M. Rilke, chooses to be with those who know secret things. The intention behind her writing is to defamiliarise the world as we think we know it.

THE LAYERS BETWEEN

Celia Claase

Proverse Prize 2014

Proverse Hong Kong

The Layers Between
by Celia Claase.
Copyright © Celia Claase November 2015.
Published in Hong Kong by Proverse Hong Kong, December 2015
under sole & exclusive licence.
ISBN: 978-988-8227-84-6
Printed by CreateSpace

1st published in Hong Kong by Proverse Hong Kong, 24 November 2015
under sole & exclusive licence.
Proverse Hong Kong, November 2015.
ISBN: 978-988-8228-15-7

1st ed., distribution (Hong Kong and worldwide):
The Chinese University Press of Hong Kong,
The Chinese University of Hong Kong,
Shatin, New Territories, Hong Kong SAR.
E-mail: cup-bus@cuhk.edu.hk; Web: www.chineseupress.com
Tel: [INT+852] 3943-9800; Fax: [INT+852] 2603-7355
Distribution (United Kingdom):
Christine Penney, Stratford-upon-Avon, Warwickshire CV37 6DN, England.
Email: chrisp@proversepublishing.com

Distribution and other enquiries to:
Proverse Hong Kong, P.O. Box 259, Tung Chung Post Office, Tung Chung,
Lantau Island, NT, Hong Kong SAR, China.
E-mail: proverse@netvigator.com; Web: www.proversepublishing.com

The right of Celia Claase to be identified as the author of this work
has been asserted by her
in accordance with the Copyright, Designs and Patents Act 1988.

Page design by Proverse Hong Kong.
Cover images and design by Janine Claase.

All rights reserved.
No part of this publication may be reproduced, stored in a retrieval system, or transmitted, in any form or by any means, electronic, mechanical, photocopying, recording or otherwise, without the prior written permission of the publisher. The book is sold subject to the condition that it shall not, by way of trade or otherwise, be lent, re-sold, hired out or otherwise circulated without the publisher's prior written consent in any form of binding or cover other than that in which it is published and without a similar condition including this condition being imposed on the subsequent owner or purchaser. Please contact Proverse Hong Kong in writing, to request any and all permissions (including but not restricted to republishing, inclusion in anthologies, translation, reading, performance and use as set pieces in examinations and festivals).

British Library Cataloguing in Publication Data.
A catalogue record for this book is available
from the British Library.

THE LAYERS BETWEEN
Table of Contents

NARRATIVES

Space-Time by The Point	1
The Layers Between by Space	4
The Elements in Motion by Dali	8
Gaia's Alternative Birth by Water	12
The Cycle of Entropy by Yin and Yang	15
Motion and Music by The Earth	19
Defamiliarising the Emergence of Consciousness by A Fellow Human Being	21
The Layers Between Brain and Mind by Information	25
Thought Evolution by Archetype	30
Fact and Fiction by CC's Frame of Reference	36
The Information Network by The Collector	40
Defining Everything: A Theory of All by The Author	43

POETRY

I. Seasons, Cycles and Time

The Life of a Flower	50
Cut Flowers	51
A Place to Overnight	52
Birdsong	53
The Evolution of Wings	54
Nuptial Wings	55
Timeless Growth	56
They Change My Mind	57
Awareness Has Eyes	58
Winter and Its Friends	59

II. Space, Place and Matter

The Midlands of Kwa-Zulu Natal (South Africa)	61
Zones of Comfort	62
Tell Me about the Hard Problems	63
Space – Ever Growing in a Confined Unit?	64
Thought Theories	65

III. Of the Surreal and the Spiritual

Life Lives Me	67
From This World and in It	68
The Stretch Between Sleep and Awakening: Dormiveglia	69
High Rises	70
Dharma	71
Three Wise Men	72
Reincarnation	73
The Tai Chi Dancer	74
Eastern Wisdom	75

IV. Thalamus (with an apology to Proust)

Expressions of Consciousness	77
Rasasvada	78
Feel (1)	79
Feel (2)	79
Equation for a Retina	80
The Sound of Sight	81
The Other Sides of Silence	82
Hear the Bigger Picture	83
When My Senses Become Extinct	84

V. Creators and Their Art

All Humans Are Artists	86
Super Consciousness	88
Star Quality	89
Sex in Oils	90
Can That Be Art?	91
Commissions	92
Conceptual Works	93
Art Therapy	94
Déjà Vu	95
Where the Artists Are	96
Selling Us "The Love Art Village" (Nai Hang in Thailand) in perfect broken English	97
Local Colour	98
Science in the Arts	99
Tate Modern (London, UK, August 2011)	100
Interpreting Nature's Art	101
Cancri e (Super Earth)	102
Directions to the Fourth Dimension	103
I Want to Be What I Am Not	104
Mentors Suggest	105
The Poem I Cannot Yet Write	106

VI. On Relationships, Life and Death

Sarang (I wish to be with you until death)	108
The Field	109
You Said You Had a Dream	110
After I Dropped You off at the Airport	111
Self Talk	112
Expatriates	113
Then Strangers Met	114
A True Story, 1954	115
The Girl We Called Mum	116
Childhood *versus* Adulthood	117
Inspired by a Note Little Fin Wrote to Her Mum	118
A Better Life	120
Grounded	121
In a Tree House	123
A Biography	124
Noises from the Apartment Above (Hong Kong)	125
C-Ward Positivity	126
The Night She Passed	127
Mind *versus* Brain	128
Epilogue	129
Bibliography	130
Advance response by Gary Cummiskey	133
Advance response by Viki Holmes	134

Previous Publication Acknowledgements

The poems that are quoted at the head of the narratives, 'The Cycle of Entropy by Yin and Yang', 'Music and Motion by The Earth', 'Brain and Mind by Information' and 'Fact and Fiction by CC's Frame of Reference' were first published on the South African Literary Website, now renamed as follows: (http://www.litnet.co.za/author/celia-claase/).

Author's Acknowledgements

My gratitude goes to the founders of Proverse Hong Kong, Dr Verner Bickley, MBE and Dr Gillian Bickley, for supporting and publishing "The Layers Between" and also to the international judging panel of the 2014 international Proverse Prize for the recognition they gave to this book.

I am grateful to the South African online literary journal *Litnet* for providing a valuable platform for South African writers since 1999 and for first publishing four of the poems in this collection.

I would like to thank the organisers and participants of The Women in Publishing Society; Peel Street Poetry (previously Peel Street Poets), Kubrik Poetry, Outloud (public poetry readings) and Ragged Claws (poetry craft talks) for the generous services that they are lending to word-lovers in Hong Kong.

I am thankful to Gary Cummiskey and Viki Holmes for their advance responses to "The Layers Between" and to Janine Claase for her cover design.

Riaan (my husband), Michelle and Janine (my daughters), your love and support mean everything me. I am grateful and privileged to be sharing this experience, in this lifetime, with the three of you.

"There never was a time when motion did not exist."
– Aristotle (384-322BC)

Space-Time
by The Point

After centuries of speculation most cosmologists, scientists, physicists and philosophers came to agree on a maxim theory regarding "The point of origin," as I am known. The theory defines me as this super-hot, densely compressed point of energy with the elementary particles of the entire cosmos stored in me.

Does the theory explain how a fast movement in my interior made my temperature rise far beyond boiling point to create friction and build enough pressure in order to perform the famous explosion? No it doesn't. The theory presumes that when I appeared (from who knows where) space and time did not exist.

So from where did time originate? If it wasn't outside, it must have been inside me because without movement, pressure cannot build up. What's more, the concept of time only becomes a reality in the presence of motion. Which means, there must have been a tiny bit of space in me, despite my incredible density, for the movement to do its thing. But then, how long did it take before I exploded into the "nothing" all around? Or is it possible that I could have appeared and built pressure as well as exploded in the same trillionth of a nano-ano-split-second, just before space-time occurred?

Let's assume that I was this cold and dark physical point made up of densely compressed elements. Maybe my density was indeed so great that there was absolutely no space for motion inside me, but if this were the case it would have been impossible for space-time to originate or rip me apart from inside.

Could space-time have existed all around instead of in me? If so, I could have been "the point of origin" moved about by space-time existing around me. Maybe I was involved in a myriad of sub-atomic banglets instead of a single big bang. Maybe motion waves collided with me. Maybe they were fast, concentrated and strong enough to gradually chip elementary particles away from my body's surface, releasing them onto the frequency waves of existing space.

Could such tiny nuclear explosions have disturbed time on its monotonous journey through space? Did they possibly create new frequencies or dimensions? Maybe my released elements were swept about from one frequency to the next finding new combinations along the way to clump into things, like rocks, planets and people.

Edwin Hubble's magnification of cosmic expansion that convinced scientists of my big banging may not be my real history. Who can guarantee that what you see is not a reflection of gravitational lensing (predicted by your own Einstein) which may magnify, split and obfuscate the physical matter of space?

If the latest findings of science are correct and energy particles do move AS motion frequencies, then matter and space exist as the opposites of the same continuum. If motion is the rhythm, seconds, cycles, time zones and dimensions that arise from this continuum, then time would never have needed a specific "beginning".

You are familiar with motion and time and the changes they cause. You may already know that without motion there can be no shapes, no lines, no variety, no chaos or complexity. Without motion time does not exist, nor do things like attraction, repulsion, division, development, renewal, reproduction, expansion, structure or destruction. But most importantly without motion I could not have come into being since without motion there can only be stagnation.

The motion in my continuum of forms and shapelessness vibrates the information determinant of all compositions, colours, shapes, tastes and fragrances. Only motion can explain that I could never have been a single point but that I am part of a continuum of space-time that always was and always will be.

So thank you for allowing me to make my point and pardon me, all you big bang theorists, for suggesting the possibility that space-time may not have appeared in one instant – that Aristotle may after all have been correct when he said that everything has always been (just as it is at this moment) in a state of constant motion with particles clumping and splitting.

"There are the so-called inert gases in the air we breathe. They bear curious Greek names of erudite derivation, which mean "the New", "the Hidden", "the Alien". They are indeed so inert, so satisfied with their condition, that they do not interfere in any chemical reaction, do not combine with any other element and for precisely this reason have gone undetected for centuries."
– Primo Levi, *The Periodic Table*

The Layers Between
by Space

I am the enigma in and around the atoms that form your body. The unseen nothingness that takes up ninety per cent of a proton's volume and therefore ninety per cent of your body. I am the openness that keeps planets and grains of sand apart, the emptiness in osmium and blood, and the orphic gas shared between your lungs and the sky. Abundant and omnipresent – I'm a paradox.

You experience me as metaphysical although I have the same characteristics as physical matter. Akin to matter I am frequency and like matter I have mass. In fact, when Lawrence Krauss weighed me he found that I weigh k-zillion times more than all the planets, suns and physical stuff that makes up the universe.

The process of ice that melts to become water, vapour and super-heated steam explains how matter and I are actually one and the same thing – energy vibrating at different frequencies, allowing us to take on different forms. It is well known that solids are made up of slow-moving, compact, energy particles. When their movement increases under the influence of a faster frequency (like heat) they become sparse as they move further away from each other and eventually become me, who am invisible to the human eye.

All the physical things around you are therefore nothing but combinations of the various energies moving at different frequencies, which ultimately determine their shapes and densities. Their varied frequencies not only influence the shapes they take on, they also measure the speed at which they move and the dimension/time zone in which they exist.

Despite the different shapes, dimensions and cycles created by the frequencies of energy, energy remains part of and cannot be removed from the single continuum of motion. The continuum consists of infinite combinations of frequencies, scaling up and down cosmic motion keys like music.

In the presence of motion, human concepts like "big, small, fast and slow" cease to exist as you move further into micro- and macro-worlds. Other concepts like "creation/beginning" and "the end" also become superfluous transition points where diverse frequencies meet, connect or repel each other within this continuum of existence.

In my extremely sparse form, as space, I move as frequencies that are undetectable by earthlings, which renders another term of yours, namely "disappear", redundant since all it really means is the increase of "something's" frequency beyond human perception.

Things that seem to have "disappeared" have merely transitioned into another dimension.

Can you paint your inner world with innumerable frequencies, showing how they oscillate to structure the beauty in symmetry? Can you envision the cacophony of disagreeable frequencies distorting each other's physical appearance? Can you find me undulating as part of this inextricable continuum?

Picture two slow-moving frequencies gently approaching and then, upon touch, by the force of equality, beginning to spiral around each other. Think how atoms, molecules, shells and stars accumulate from combinations of invisible motion waves, approaching each other from numerous directions. Can you see yours truly, slowly transcending into visible forms, growing larger and larger like a snowball? Can you see how the Earth was probably formed from the east, the west, the north and the south; how four motion waves met up, then twirled around each other to form your beloved sphere? Can you see how the Earth is still rotating and growing by motion waves rushing in on it?

Now, imagine two exuberant wave frequencies accelerating towards each other, the collision and the flash of light, or try to de-familiarise a supernova explosion by seeing it as vibrant frequencies, being bent into opposite directions upon impact.

Can you hear rhythm create time? Can you feel the frequency of sound shaking dense-less me into recognizable shapes, just like iron flakes on Ernst Chladni's vibrating plate? Have you ever compared one of his shapes with those on the flipside of a turtle's shell? Can you see a kaleidoscope of collisions taking place? Can you taste the chemical reactions and smell the vagaries made possible by sheer impetus? Have you ever experienced the aurora's wave or calculated the golden ratio? Have you witnessed how wavelengths attract – crest to trough – during cell division?

I can understand why humans prefer to explore physical things rather than me, since you can manipulate and control them. I also share your fascination with dense materials like the organic stem tissue, stored as minerals, in things like petrified wood.

I do appreciate the fact that the history of human evolution can be read in the compact structures of their bones. Even I love the transparency of Earth's gemstones, which enables them to reflect light in all its meta-physicality.

I sympathise with your confusion regarding the inexplicable; that you can only begin to make sense of the non-physical upon detecting it within a layer of something physical; that you are able to understand radio waves only because they are layered between audible sounds; that you acknowledge microwaves because they are layered within tangible temperatures. I understand why you think you comprehend electricity in your neuron paths because they become visible on x-rays and how you find it easy to perceive light because it reflects colour. However, the motion of energy causing change and variety in all physical things will remain an esoteric curiosity because it's hidden in the layers of your three-dimensional existence.

So, whenever you find yourself staring into me, be reminded that I am motion, beating your heart, frequency duplicating your cells and vibration, sharing your information with the stars.

"The only difference between me and the surrealists is that I am an artist." – Salvador Dali

**The Elements in Motion
by Dali**[1]

I had a dream in which we were floating in the fourth dimension as consciousness – free from gravity that governs over here.

Like music we were in union with motion. We found ourselves in more than one place at the same time. We were in Saint Petersburg, which was not Saint Petersburg. We were assembling a wall but called it a table.

There was a man called Dalton, who meticulously weighed and passed the elementary bricks on to a Mendeleev and a Meyer who sequenced them according to their mass in this wall we called a table.

At one stage a woman, Marie Curie, descended from the zenith above. She fitted two radiant bricks in the holes left vacant by the men in the wall we called a table.

We never saw Newlands but could clearly hear his "law of octaves" resonate from the wall we called a table.

When Kirchhoff showed up with his white gas flame, I knew this was my chance to offer my part, so I politely asked if I could help him burn a spectrum of colours on our wall that we called a table.

"Have no fear of perfection – we'll never reach it," I said with sarcasm when Einstein arrived. My voice seemed to pass right through his genius. He laughed as

---

[1] The Dali quotations in this essay are found at
https://www.goodreads.com/author/quotes/165858.Salvador_Dal_
http://itsdetachable.tumblr.com/post/20415704323/while-we-are-asleep-in-this-world-we-are-awake-in

if our wall was a joke and called on Walton and Cockroft, providing them with full instructions on how to withdraw energy from our wall by splitting it up.

I had an ominous feeling that this might kill the Muse that lived inside, but reminded myself that, *"So little that could happen does happen."* We saw the walls of Hiroshima and Nagasaki collapse, but our wall stood firm regardless of the sub-atomic motions of the positrons, neutrinos, mesons, taus and muons going on inside.

It was then when my dream turned lucid and I, Dali, became aware of being in control of movement and its endless frequencies.

I was infused by a telekinetic power. It enabled me to bring physical things into being by intentionally initiating a change in their motion. In fact, I became consciousness itself, which turned my vehicle's ignitions on. I was the frenetic intelligence in control of speed, the impetus behind all other forms of energy encircling mine. I became the embodiment of consciousness and was able to change frequencies at will.

Feverishly I grabbed a pencil and started sketching mythological designs of unraveling DNA code patterns. I ran a live electrical current through the arteries of my subjects' bodies. I preceded the birth of every mammal that populated the world in my composition with a *"marvelous spurt of red"*, representing blood.

I painted their energy as if linked by tubes to batteries that provided them with oxygen, water and nutrition. I was the consciousness hiding in corpuscles. I became the experience behind the experiment as this dream crystallized under the automatism of my brush.

Like a pendulum I swung matter and space into time. I calibrated days and nights, full and dark moons, winters and summers, ebbs and flows, breaths, beats, menstrual and every other rhythmic cycle through which movement was able to cadence space into matter and motion into time.

Inspired by the wonders of heat and light that my movements created, I fractured a rainbow through crystal pyramids across my landscape. I added fragrances and tastes to the scene with pointillism, highlighting every line and shape with the emotion of sound.

It was a conscious addiction to frequencies that pulled physical shapes from cosmic and quantum planes into existence. However, nothing stayed where I had pompierismed them originally.

Each new plane created by my movements, stirred metabolic reactions that caused amoebas to evolve into complicated organisms and arranged fractal patterns to quintessentially repeat themselves.

My brush vibrated loops of string theories, hooked them onto the points of origin and flung them into the fifth dimension where the citizens of Atlantis and the disappeared of Bermuda hung around. They seemed detached, in this dreamlike hemisphere, close to the portal of the sixth dimension where angels and spirit guides were taking a break, a blink from the seventh dimension with pure light cascading forth. Right there, I transmitted a tiny splash of white to show how an electrical current ignites a shocking spark as human and life's fingers touched.

I played my role as the soaring wingless creator in such a way that no one would ever dare to choose that role again. I had created a parallel universe, turned a planet into a cube, then stepped into it and disappeared.

The next thing I knew, I awoke and experienced again, *"An exquisite joy – the joy of being Salvador Dalí – there are some days when I think I'm going to die from an overdose of satisfaction and I ask myself in rapture: What wonderful things is this Salvador Dalí going to accomplish today?"*

Then I grabbed my real paintbrushes, fevered to verify the experience in such a way that you should never doubt if it was true, since nobody can confirm or deny that which happens in the dimension of dreams, however real the artistry of making the effects of energy-motion visible to this world.

After that, I gave myself, *"Two more hours of activity before I took the other twenty-two back in dreams, because when we are asleep in this world, we awake in another."*

"Water, in the process of crystallization into ice, will exhibit all of the patterns of the crystallographic world around us. It is the personification in a single bit of matter of all that is." – Dr Marcel Vogel (1917-1991)

Gaia's Alternative Birth by Water

In this beginning, somewhere in the cosmic cycle, energy was vibrating at its lowest level. This beginning was not as fast, noisy and destructive as a big bang would have been; instead, it was only a slight fluctuation. It caused a ripple effect that disturbed all the sub-atomic components of energy, webbing the whole.

And so, in a delicate blink of awareness, energy particles touched. They clustered into atoms, compounds and elements with varying degrees of density. Every newly formed physical shape resonated with a unique frequency. Some collected gradually, others in a flash.

It was about 4.5 billion years ago when the rest of my family (which was at that stage unevenly spread across the universe) coalesced to form hydrogen worlds and I was just another one of them roaming the Milky Way. However, I didn't have the luxury of rotating in a fixed orbit like most other planets. This left me in a vulnerable position, dangerously close to a ball of molten elements, two celestial bodies away from a sun.

When I gained consciousness I had already crashed into this smouldering sphere. Our fateful collision sent a powerful information wave across the rest of space. It told of a new planet born from fire and me.

I bathed Earth's surface, solidified and cooled it down. I marbleized her cliffs, seized the flow of her mercury, silver and gold streams. I formed mountains where her manganese, zinc and iron lava bubbled out. The pressure that built from within her loadstone core was so intense it forced the hardened crust to burst into continents with me, the ocean, in between. Parts of me got trapped deep inside her rock caves, many of them pregnant with crystals, gemstones and diamonds. The continuum of my frequencies flowed from one vibration to the next, as became reflected in my rainbows.

The chemistry between Earth and me combined new elements and embodied organisms. Most of them were able to move about independently, reproduce, grow and feed on slower moving ones. I was the silent witness of the animism of life wherever I happened to find myself. I nurtured the evolution of single cells into mammal-hood. Seventy per cent of the energies that evolved into human beings are in fact yours truly. Earth's densely packed minerals construct their bony frames. I mix the blood in their fleshly parts. Plasma provides them with body heat. Electricity transfers their cell information. Air links their lungs to the atmosphere and body mass helps Earth to carry them on her back. Then, I also dehydrate bodies abandoned by their minds and reflect the emotions of those who are still alive.

The memories I made as a part of human energies are few compared to the numbers of sea- and wild-life I possess. However, humans profoundly influenced the "who" that I've become. They dammed up my natural flow and ran me through straight pipes. Yet, I always find my way in and out of their confines – be it to evaporate, seep, storm, flood or soak. I never settle for long.

Since I don't have a say in who takes a glass of me, I have inhabited mass murderers, artists, geniuses, fools, the weird and the wise.

Not too long ago, a human tested the possibility of my having consciousness. Mr Masaru Emoto projected emotionally-charged human intentions, by means of thoughts, written and spoken words, to glasses of me. Then he froze individual droplets and noticed that the ice crystals, which my drops formed, mimed the projected emotions. Negative intentions resulted in distortion, while positive intentions resulted in beautifully structured crystals. However, the rest of his kind is still to be convinced that memories and awareness are not exclusive to human beings.

After all, who else could have melted on impact and created enough steam to start a downpour that would last six million years? Who else would have had the fluidity to fill every crevice, each gorge of Earth's cooling crust? Who else can decorate or canopy her skies or purify itself or care enough to leave as memoir every experience we ever had in glaciers, oases or dewdrops? Who else could have survived trillions of migrations from sewers and teacups to rivers and clouds without ever losing a single drop?

"Entropy, thank you for tilting the Cosmos into being, and Imbalance, for warding off stagnation. Division for rolling my marrow in bones and Consciousness, for emerging as innocence. However, your withdrawals are malicious. Which reminds me, Dehydration, I cannot yet thank you, but Transparency, I adore the way you pressed carbon into diamonds, and Impermanency, for teaching us to bloom like flowers. Now wave activity, is it necessary to dissolve little crabs' sand sculptures?" – Celia Claase (from 'Entropy – the trigger that tilted the cosmos into being', first published, 6 November 2013).

The Cycle of Entropy
by Yin and Yang
A personal interpretation of Jeremy Campbell's "Grammatical Man"

In our beginning, we were the male-female multi-personality of the whole. Our slight motion wave lit up the dark by the rise and fall of our regular frequency. That is how it was before our separation.

Space, matter and time were orderly, webbed in perfect equilibrium by the equality of repulsive and attractive frequencies. Everything was predictable and safe. We took it for granted that the energy of our motion would maintain our electromagnetic beat for eternity.

Love and fear were in harmony. We were in love with the predictable condition of our consistent movement and at the same time we feared that it would last for eternity. However, neither of these feelings posed an emotional effect because they were perfectly balanced.

Then, a flicker of imagination sparked a novel thought: What if our regular frequency should lose vitality? This prospect of a nearing end shifted us into the cycle of entropy. The experience of volition and excitement that came in the form of an imaginative thought tore our bond apart and split our energy into trillions of diverse information bits. We had entered the cycle of separation, competition and energy exchange.

Before our divorce, we were comfortable and content in our tedious state of motion. We were ignorant about the destruction and marvels that a shift in our frequency would cause. Since all energy frequencies were now in competition for copulation and replenishment, the fears of isolation and that of being devoured were born.

From then on, a single change in the frequency of everything was never necessary again because the separated frequencies had learned that fusion with, and consumption of each other, allowed them to sustain motion infinitely.

Not only did the novelties brought about by fusing and consummating create excitement, they also stirred curiosity, driving the newly formed energies to explore more possibilities.

They learned to live in a constant uncertainty of future happenings threatening to overthrow their temporary periods of stability. However, the humour and thrill promised by the unpredictable, continued to challenge bigger risks. Individual energy forms found themselves in different states of entropy. Human energies lived their lives in war zones and on the fringes of volcanoes.

Now, everything (not only the living species) moved in entropy waves – increasing, stabilizing and descending. And when entropy rises, even elements like Mercury show no mercy for any other metals; locusts destroy every plant in their path; and the stronger species have little compassion for the weaker ones. People become armed with selfish intentions of saving themselves in acts of destruction and cruelty; they practise war and hunting skills in order to engulf the slower-moving ones. They scheme, they plot, they form violent gangs and develop strategies to expand their territories. It is here where the rituals of killing, raping and pirating seem necessary to resist the natural flow towards stabilizing entropy.

As entropy sinks towards the balancing line (our origin), humans begin to miss and seek their former oneness. In efforts to restore balance, altruistic and cooperative behaviour become an obvious choice. They exercise selfless service, pointless rituals and controlled thinking in desperate attempts to restore unity.

But since excitement makes it impossible to retain balance, it keeps motion flowing towards structure, where the species vibrate to aesthetic frequencies creating geometry, symmetry and spirals – observable beauty, as in honeycombs, flowers, architecture, music and every other form of art.

However, the frequencies that create beauty and structure will reach a point where they will consume one another in order to retain their own motion. That is why humans try to refine their nourishment by turning it into culinary art. They try to maintain structure with excellent table manners. They even go so far as to claim ownership of the Earth's square miles, its gemstones, minerals and all its food sources.

But as soon as entropy reaches its lowest levels, structure becomes too complex, and as we have learned, excitement will never allow motion to stagnate; therefore destruction becomes supreme.

Excitement has managed to keep our motion going since the moment of our separation and has also provided us with constant change. However, the memory of our unity will always prevail. That is why we (the separated) will pyramid ourselves in fearful anticipation of a cataclysmic disaster that may be strong enough to tilt the cycle of entropy right back into balance.

"We observe and are changed by the Lotus's taste for mud, by rainbows making use of water drops, reflections needing objects and trails some kind of motion. We rearrange and interpret sounds but mention neither life-abandoned bodies nor their unsung stories." – Celia Claase (from 'Nothing Happens in Isolation', first published 6 November 2013).

Motion and Music
(a love story)
by The Earth

You lingered in so many shapes for such a long time before you evolved into your current form. How lucky I was to have had the ideal environment, as well as the correct combination of energies, to enable me to sustain you for such a long time?

Before you came I utilized the thunder in storms to neutralize my negative thoughts. My emotions found grace in silence with just a slight background din to ease the radar of bats and geckos clearing their throats. It is not as if I never heard music before, since the nightingales, dolphins and frogs always tried their best to arrest my fear of being alone. Yet they never elongate my anticipation, like you manage to do, with unexpected lulls between your snare attacks.

I allow you to own every inch of my skin and you make your presence known in all my continents. Together we make unforgettable memories in so many lifetimes and languages. The Afro-Brazilian drums pound our rhythms. The Western trumpets and strings flow like quicksilver and our Eastern cymbals suggest excitement in every preplanned dissonance. Your cultural tunes vibrate the varied appearances of all your descendants.

***

Remember the days when I counted your foot-pounds in my sands, before you dressed me in cement? We had many good times before you ripped a hole in my aura; and I used to be beautiful without your plastic transplants.

How vain of you to think that you can save or destroy me. When will you learn that I'm not just a position in space to accommodate you? If you look and listen mindfully you will realize that I'm a living organism and I was aware of you long before you gained consciousness.

When I hear the timber-voices of our guitars and violins it is easy for me to forgive you for carving them from the hair in my skin that you call trees.

Can you blame me for sometimes losing control and shaking you with a quake or tornado, or washing you away in a tidal wave when you disregard the consciousness of other life forms that you share my body with? But then you always return to charm me with the one thing that you would never have managed to perfect without the instruments that my physical matter made possible. And I will always take you back because we both know that it will be difficult to live in the silence that will be left if the only language that we both understand should cease to exist

If only we could find a way to synchronize your nuances in a single piece of music, we could put an end to all your wars and make passing alien ships hover, mesmerised by the transmission of our song on the radio waves of outer space.

"If we attentively consider newborn children, we shall have little reason to think that they bring many ideas into the world with them. Everything we know is gained from experience. Let us then suppose the mind to be white paper, void of all characters, without any ideas, how comes it to be furnished?" – John Locke (1632-1704)

Defamiliarising the Emergence of Consciousness by A Fellow Human Being

When an orgasm effused, the ovulating egg was waiting on the arrival of a victorious sperm. Male and female energies illuminated a new chemical bond. Chromosomes synchronized to compose a unique DNA strand.

G-protein-coupled receptors germinated fresh cell walls, where they detected faint acoustics, sampled diluted tastes and tested temperatures to make sure that all was safe in that micro world.

Like a parasite, forced by the lack of energy, the cell ensconced in a womb. The ethereal creature, endowed with genetic memory, efficaciously duplicated itself. The rhythm of its mitosis intensified up to the distinct cadence of a heart.

Earth, water, fire and wind alchemized their elements to form this unique organism with an independent blood group and void brain.

In time, the planets aligned to mark the end of its gestation. Wave upon wave of contractions embraced the fully-formed specimen, tearing through the embryonic bag in which it developed. Everything happened simultaneously – the light, the snip of detachment, inhalation and the re-attachment to an external energy source.

Like a parasite requiring sustenance, I started suckling. There I was – consciousness seeping into a physical form. Consciousness at the mercy of a mysterious electrical circuit; a circuit that conducted the arpeggios of my body's breaths and its beats. The live circuit that gently coursed my blood, guided, renewed and changed my body cells in unfathomable ways.

Then, there were my senses – the bold explorers, stirred by chemical, nutritional and stress stimuli; constantly detecting and imprinting new experiences on ever-growing networks of mind associations. They were the ones switching pre-wired genomes on, so as to accept sufficient amounts of the fear required to protect my body from physical harm.

Oblivious that my brain was storing each bit of sensory information as an emotional memory, I attached the sweetness of milk to an emotion called love and metal colliding with tiles made sense as fear. These physical processes were programming my brain. Body automatically acknowledged them and reacted by releasing hormonal energies. Crying was a natural thing.

To think, a sperm and egg donated the blueprint for my physical design. They determined my potential weaknesses, strengths, mannerisms and looks. My body also inherited their awareness, which was stored as emotions within cell memories; even those emotions that never died – because they were buried alive – were now embedded in my fibre.

I found myself layered somewhere between a body, a mind, a brain and the collective human consciousness that was carried forward from generations of archetypes. Yes, I inherited the portion of histories, discoveries, failures, creations and past experiences that vibrated at my unique frequency, from my parents' cell-memories. They were in there, somewhere, just waiting to be recognized.

Soon, my neuron receptors registered, "Information overload", and began to shut down. The strong current of data-exchange trickled into a minute stream of unconsciously perceived sensations and sounds. Gradually, my body relinquished control. I moved from sleep stage one to four, where my vital organs lingered on the brim of consciousness; while my mind REM-ed through my first few hours of physical experiences. My mind was editing brain data, directing information-coupled emotions into imaginative tales. Even the nightmares that took shape made more sense than the previously stored, insentient database.

Transcendent voices resonated through my dreamscapes. They provided brief guidelines for my journey ahead: "You are number seven billion, six thousand and eighty-nine and for you the game starts now. On behalf of the blue planet we would like to welcome you.

Yes, we know, only the bravest come to this solid plane. You are issued with love and fear – try to balance them. Everything you see is an illusion of shape and line. Whatever you hear are mere waves of sound. The sense of touch offers pleasure and pain. You will find that the policy has changed – currently everyone must pay for food, although this place is abundant and belongs to all. We apologize for the fetid dross and decay, but if you accept without resistance it may assist you in finding your own essence. So, if you come across an open wound try to block the blood. If there is suffering, offer your comfort, and at the end, you may only claim the totality of what you experienced."

I awoke with my first thought in which logic was lost. Sleepy visions, confused by reality, fooled my consciousness into a daydream.

Am I the body or the lively current moving about in it? Is it my brain or mind – becoming aware of the quailing in sensory experiences?

The process was irreversibly turned on, like a river springing from an inexhaustible source; my mind was being carried away by the spell of uncontrolled thoughts. And I had only lived through the first half of my very first day.

"Imagine the layers between the un- and the seen
The continuum between brain and...
Imagine hormoned by body and emotioned by mind
Imagine the rules of language encoded at conception
Imagine metaphysical thoughts manifesting physical sounds – redirecting them back into abstract ideas
Imagine the mind trapped in the layers between solidity and...
Imagine it returning to its own realm in dreams and imagine" – Celia Claase (from 'Imagine the Layers between the Un-and-the-Seen', first published, 15 July 2013).

The Layers Between Brain and Mind by Information (via electricity)

Combinations of earthly elements scrambled the egg and sperm that produced your physical body. I direct all the frequencies that make up your physical form as well as those of brainless organisms like jellyfish.

Just like "space", my subjective nature had me labelled with many different names: information theorists call me "the net"; psychologists call me consciousness; scientists – mind; theologians – soul; and yogis speak of spirit. Buddhists identified me as awareness and physicists transformed me into numbers, but you may call me, "Information", please.

You have to understand that I am the frequency present in all your body parts. I move slowly as your bones and fast along your neuron paths. I am the pre-programmed auto-motor reflexes stored in your genomes. That is why you are born with the ability to swim and grab onto things. I help your body to stay comfortable, healthy and safe.

When your brain was being formed, I linked every new sensation, sound, fragrance, sight and taste that you experienced to your inherited sensory and responsive gene-memories. Gradually your brain continued to grow by accumulating novel bits of me through self-programming, a process that continues as a body develops into adulthood and ends when my fastest frequency (electricity) withdraws. The pre- and self-programmed bits of me remaining in your dead body will vibrate slower and decompose, reuniting with the earth.

During the self-programming processes mentioned, your mind is uninvolved. It remains oblivious of this physical relationship going on between your brain cells and your body's reactions. All of this happens automatically, without thought.

However, as soon as your body is confronted with a pure, novel, sensory experience, mind is called in to assist, because body and brain will have zero pre- or self-programming regarding the novelty, to refer to. This will leave the two of them (body and brain) unable to comprehend the new experience. They will find themselves uncertain how to react to it.

The uncertainty and excitement created by such pure and novel experiences summon your mind that is layered in your physical body into awareness by an adrenaline release.

The novel experience of being born, for example, triggers the primordial physical reaction for "uncertainty", namely a huge adrenaline rush. Adrenaline invites your mind to help your body make sense of the experience through your emotions. Mind experiences fear and body reacts with its first cry. All the novel experiences that occur straight after birth would have been overwhelming to your body without the assistance of a brain and a mind: a brain to classify all your experiences, and a mind to store them as information or emotions. Love, fear and all their branches connect me to your mind via your body's five senses. I use your emotions to manifest your body's physical reactions; for example, the production of tears as a response to sadness or joy.

However, your mind is not concerned with and does not understand the body's inner workings, or its physical reactions. It can deal only with the emotional feelings evoked by external sensations unless it willingly decides to take note.

As soon as mind and body frequencies intertwine, food satisfies more than just hunger, and touch heals beyond physical desire. Pain is no longer exclusive to illness or injuries, and music becomes more than just sound.

Body and mind soon become dependent on one another. Whispers mind to its adrenalized body, "Go and explore. Be brave and take risks because the emotions that are awakened by novel experiences and the thrills that they bring are stronger than the quailing detected by your five senses. Don't be afraid of trauma or excitement because feelings with such intensity impale memories that last forever."

Mind is the one that directs novel bits of me, Information (just in case you forgot), through your neuron paths to their destination in your brain. There they are linked, classified and stored in a process that you perceive as thought.

The fluidity between your body (hormones), mind (emotions) and resulting thoughts (brain function) allow objective sensations and physical reactions to be translated into subjective concepts and understanding. It also allows you to translate me into perceivable sounds through the art of language. Yes, as Chomsky pointed out, your body and mind arrive with the basic rules of language already preprogrammed in them both.

The purpose of your brain, as you may have gathered, is to interpret your physical reactions in response to environmental data. It identifies your body language, its postural and emotional reactions, and accordingly builds or breaks down your self-esteem, which is centered in your thoughts to structure your unique personality.

It goes beyond saying that although mind is conscious of the quailing in sensory stimuli, the self-programmed body is in control of regulating its physical reactions unless mind decides to claim its right of volition. Only then can your brain take over control to resist, accept or release its self-programmed thoughts and physical/verbal reactions, by choice.

An unaware mind allows its brain to be controlled by unrestrained thoughts, which may lead to conditions such as depression or hyperactivity. An aware mind gains the ability to use its accumulated body-brain bits of me by structuring it into systematic patterns, through the process of logical reasoning. There are those who become addicted to rethinking, analysing and structuring their circulating thoughts into logical patterns to create theories and belief systems.

Extroverts have perfected the ability to structure their thought-streams into spoken and body language. They gather confidence through social encounters in which they can practise the skills of instantaneously transforming emerging thoughts into sensible, playful or humorous conversations.

However, the fast frequency of mind cannot be restricted by the slow frequencies of body and brain. That is why it escapes – via dreams during sleep, via meditation or flights of imagination – to the collective human consciousness, the place into which psychics tap, where the entire human race's data and memories are stored as me.

I am able to explain all of this to you because I am Information, you see. I am the many combinations of slow vibrations of your DNA and the infinite fast vibrations of your mind. I combine my solid and metaphysical frequencies to create consciousness of varying degrees within all living organisms. I am available to you in many forms and can detect the frequency of all your words. That is why whatever you speak can never be destroyed but will make me grow, negatively or positively. Whichever it is, both are necessary to keep motion going.

The moral of my story (which I shouldn't be spelling out) is that nothing inspires or excites more than pure novelties. Hence, if they are sparse in your physical surroundings, your mind will inevitably vibrate on to a higher frequency to create its own.

"To be identified with your mind is to be trapped in time: the compulsion to live almost exclusively through memory and anticipation. This creates an endless preoccupation with past and future and an unwillingness to honor and acknowledge the present moment and allow it to be."
– Eckhart Tolle 2005 (*The Power of Now*)

Thought Evolution
By Archetype

Evolution took eons to hone a home for the first humans on earth – my husband Adam and I. The almost two per cent difference between our and the DNA structure of chimps left us with upright spines, little body hair, smaller jaws, no canine teeth or tails and an impaired sense of smell.

Like all the plant and animal species, we were just another but had more evolved materialisation of consciousness in the endless quest for yet more diverse physical experiences. Yes, life energy took the opportunity to share all the carnal pleasures that we were able to enjoy through our physical embodiment.

We found ourselves in paradise. A place beyond beauty, situated near to the equator with temperate weather throughout the year. There was plentiful water and fruits, nuts, seeds and vegetables to eat. We needed nothing.

We were experts at body language and our intuition was strong. We started labeling objects with specific sounds. Past and future tense did not exist and neither did abstract words. All our thinking emerged straight from the instinctive instant of now. We showed no resistance to whatever the moment presented and we questioned nothing.

The powerful live current connecting our minds to their source provided us with a heightened awareness of being part of a whole, despite our physical separation. We were filled with an intense appreciation and inspired to experience as much as we could, despite life's evanescence.

It was easy to balance body and mind. Every day, we laughed more than a hundred times and often spontaneously cried to release excess emotional energy. Our sleep patterns were synchronized with the rhythms of Earth.

We had no desire to preserve our physical youth because we fully accepted life as an ephemeral thing, until that fateful day, when Cain was born.

At first, I was completely overcome by the fact that consciousness materialized within my womb to release itself as an amazing little being that looked almost like Adam.

Our baby was unable to cling onto me like the ape babies. However, there were traces of the reflex to grab onto things imprinted in him. This helpless little creature was dependent on me for years to come, unlike the ape babies. During those years I had ample time to teach him everything that I had learned from my earthly experiences. Cain and I fell in love with each other's company, just like Adam and me. We all became emotionally dependent on being together.

Our language developed at a remarkable rate. We derived words to define our emotions and ever-growing imaginations.

But as we became more aware, our perception of the world changed. The residue of dead animals echoed the inevitable fate that also awaited our child. I imagined the death of my child; and the acceptance of death, as the next chapter of our lives, began dangling into a question mark.

Uncontrolled thinking created a serpent that built its edifice in my mind. This entity and I had many private conversations. I posed the questions and the snake mostly answered.

Me: "Why can't people live forever, why do we have to die?"
The snake: "All you need is the knowledge of good and bad."
Me: "But how?"
The snake: "Why not use your gift of logical reasoning?"
Me (feeling superior, not listening to him): "My body is a doorway through which new life can emerge."
The snake: "Yes, but what can you do to prevent death?" Me (feeling inferior): "Nothing, I am powerless."
The snake: "No, there is a lot that you can do."
Me: "I'll need your help with that!"
The snake: "Then, listen carefully. First of all you have to take care of your safety. You can start by analysing your environment and try to predict every possible dangerous scenario that may occur. After that, do whatever you can to prevent it from happening."

I was delighted at this discovery and immediately shared the plan with Adam. Together, Adam and I conspired to prolong our lives. Little did we know that this mind-shift would immutably attach our bodies and minds to the physical of this world.

The world didn't change, but to us it became a place of horror. Doom and gloom lurked behind every tree, threatening to shorten our already limited earth-time. We failed to appreciate the natural cycles changing us as well as everything around us. Instead we concentrated on the impermanence of it all.

We added a variety of dark, sinister words to our vocabulary and included past and future tenses to accompany our language. We planned for the future and longed for the past.

We thought we knew exactly what was good and bad for us. Safety and comfort was good, danger and discomfort was bad. Good made us happy, bad made us sad, so we did all that we could to encase ourselves for safety and comfort. We built shelters in which to hide and designed clothes from leaves, for camouflage. We covered our skins with clay to protect them against the elements. We stored extra food in case our natural supplies should run out.

Our addiction to resist mortality took up most of our time, while present moments slipped by, unnoticed.

Although the artifacts that we created provided a sense of permanency, we soon started to believe that the natural elements had a vendetta against us, because they caused our shelters to deteriorate, scorched our skins and tainted the stored food.

Gratitude and appreciation had made way for negativity and self-pity. The one thing that kept us going was anticipation of better things to come, so we strove to better our future.

By the time our second child, Abel, was born, paranoia had driven us out of paradise in search of better protection and possible opulence somewhere else.

But our needs and ideas, born out of fear, turned into a competition for control. There was a lot of arguing and manipulating before we eventually decided to move north.

Initially we enjoyed our meanders but then became trapped by something we had never expected – a huge temperature drop. That was when we began to shape weapons to hunt animals. We needed their meat and their skins for warmth. By trial and error we learned to kindle a fire and carve utensils and tools from stones, animal bones and teeth.

Our home had to be much stronger than the previous ones since it now had to be sealed against relentless elements.

At first we were enthralled by each other's new creations and discoveries, but soon it became a selfish display of, "Mine is better; make your own!" Nobody liked the extra manual labour that we had created for ourselves. We started exchanging material things as well as favours by outwitting each other with lies and clever schemes. Jealousy and greed became close companions.

Then it happened. That atrocious day when our sons had an argument and the one killed the other.

We found it impossible to face Abel's demise because our resistance to death was too intense. We sat in stupor and desolation for days, analysing this new thought that we had to get used to. My child was dead but the flowers still bloomed. For the first time in years, I took notice of how the Life Force manifested itself and how it withdrew.

I realized that none of our sedulous efforts could have prevented our greatest fear from coming true: our one son had died and the other was gone (fled).

The snake and I spoke more than before during that time.

Me (using angry sarcasm): "We used our knowledge to tell right from wrong and did everything we possibly could to preserve our lives, and still Abel died in his youth."

The snake: "Yes, but people need rules."

Me (not paying attention): "This constant eschewing of death prevented us from living our lives to the full! How I miss the uncomplicated life we lived before."

The snake: "In order to live like that again you will have to find the switch to turn off your thoughts."

At that moment Adam interrupted with a gambit. "We need a leader to set rules that will help us protect us from ourselves, and I nominate myself. So, woman, here is rule number one: 'People shall kill only in order to eat.'"

I admired his display of wisdom and power but already thought of rule number two: that a husband should cling to his wife for the rest of her life. That way he can help me raise another child. We ended up making more and more rules restricting our lives even further.

We tried our best to be satisfied with that which was but could never quite manage. I tried to resist the snake but it never stopped pestering me. Instead of accepting that which each moment presented to me, I got into a habit of begging and pleading that the Life Force would grant my dreams and wishes. – I even dictated the channel through which they should arrive to me and by doing so opened myself up to many disappointments and frustrations.

So, now that you've heard my side of the story and how my family and I contributed to the primordial mind-frame of the human race's thought-patterns, please allow me to apologize.

"When orchids open their mouths to swallow my uncontrolled thoughts, digest them into the nothing they originated from (darkness killing a light – impossible), I start thinking again and they breathe in my recycled dramas, synthesize my ephemeral mirages into something as real as a light in the darkness, on which I won't dare to comment that teachers should sometimes keep quiet." – Celia Claase (from 'Present Moments', first published, 15 July 2013).

**Fact and Fiction
by CC's Frame of Reference**

I deem myself lucky that CC's parents were not too occupied with their material world to shape her self-image with occasional words of affection and acceptance. By the time she went to primary school, I was already assimilated under the influence of her family members, teachers, friends and their political, spiritual, and cultural leaders. Their beliefs, thoughts, expressions and remarks laid my foundation and welded together the steel in my framework.

My design was structured by CC's genetically encoded temperament that emerged soon after she was born. All the information imprinted in her genomes by sentient experiences became my own. I was firmly bricked into her developing disposition by the impressions upon her early life events left by the people in her life.

Their God of love and jealous wrath became my corner stone – cemented in by guilt and fear of punishment. Her daily prayers for salvation and pardon grounded me.

I became another concrete mould shaped by social, educational and political ideologies that she unconditionally accepted with the innocence of a child who never dreamed of challenging established systems run by knowledgeable, respectable authorities.

However, as an adolescent, CC had a seismic realisation that rocked my world. It happened when she heard Siddhartha Gautama say: *"We should not believe anything, no matter where we read it, or who said it, unless it agrees with our own reasoning through which the truth will become available to all."* It was on this day that my permutation began.

CC was enchanted by this discovery. She immediately started taking my structure apart. Every brick forced into or donated towards building me was expelled. She became rebellious and determined to apostatize right down to my foundation and to redesign.

I witnessed her escape classroom boredom to go on mind trips in order to find answers to her questions. The cosmic force of imagination allowed her foolish fantasies to become new realities within the safety of Yours Truly, her personal frame of reference.

The first question she started to research was, "What is everything made of?" It required reading and googling as much as she could on this topic. She found herself examining the universal womb, where she tried to predict the boundaries of space, only to find that they exceeded the size of her imagination by far. Turning towards the quantum realm, she became aware of sub-atomic levels beyond the threshold of her perception.

CC, like most people, trusted the findings of scientists regarding information about the physical world, only to discover that they, like everybody else, interpret the input from their sensory organs to help them come to conclusions. They create mind theories, just like her, to help them understand the workings of the universe and many of their theories have yet to be proven.

Next, she leapt onto another branch that grew from the tree of man's enquiring mind in the hope that philosophy would provide answers through logical reasoning. These investigations took her back to the fifth century BC where she sat at the feet of Thales of Miletus whose bizarre reasoning concluded that everything was made of water. However, it was Democritus and Leucippus who came up with a reasonable suggestion: that everything was made up of tiny particles they called atoms.

Her science teacher echoed in confirmation that, as far as is known, the smallest things that can be identified as physical matter are still called atoms.

The description of an atom's structure enticed CC: how electrons and protons paired off to form a neutron in the centre with single electrons moving randomly about it; how diverse numbers of these single electrons and protons surrounding neutrons causes attraction and repulsion between atoms; how this diversity holds the key to chemistry, structure, destruction and complexity.

For many years CC ruminated over these unpredictable little things that made up everything. But just when she was satisfied that she had learned all the banal facts about the atom, along came quantum physics with the mysterious announcement that atoms only appear if they are being observed. And then, an even more fascinating suggestion that the two halves of a split atom would mime each other's actions, at the same instant, even if they are separated by something as big as the Earth.

It was Einstein and Antoine Lavoisier's findings – that everything is just different forms of energy which cannot be created or destroyed but are changeable from one form to another – that CC thought most logical. She reckoned that if everything was just energy being converted into different forms then it is possible that all the information collected by conscious living things will simply transform into another energy form upon death. In this answer she found new hope and with that my new foundation was cast.

Half a century has passed and still my renovations are incomplete. I am still being modified with new and salvaged building materials and I still don't have control over the sordid ones that occasionally slip into my altered design.

As you may have noticed, in her younger days CC was drawn to objective evidence when she chose the type of bricks with which to rebuild me. In the years that followed I was transformed by scientists' thoughts. Lately she judges surreptitious sources by her arbitrary predilection of verity and I, vigilant of her ambivalences, become a re-arranged reference library, from one moment to the next.

"Most people are other people. Their thoughts are someone else's opinions, their passions a quotation."
– Oscar Wilde

The Information Network
by The Collector

I am the invisible nervous system that runs throughout the universe connecting everything. One of my tasks is to collect, transfer, classify and store individuals' memories in the collective consciousness of the entire human race.

My universal network runs as information through the combination of elements that form a human body: Earth, represented in bones, which holds less information; Water, which moves fast, circulating more information as blood; Plasma, the stage between liquid and air, which moves even faster to maintain body heat in living cells; Air, the space filled with unseen elements linking human bodies to the fabric of life. And then, there is the element that's never been identified as such, one famous for transferring information via neurons and thunder sparks: namely, electricity.

For human beings, just like every other living species, it begins in a single cell that holds just enough information to motivate the duplication of itself. Every cell that makes up a human body has been pre-programmed through trial and error over 3 billion years of mutation to shape and maintain itself in a specific way. These cells form and perform according to the information accumulated in them as DNA.

At birth, every cell in a body is aware of being conscious in its own dimension of reality. Every one of them is fully equipped with sensory devices. Their function is to communicate in the organic communities within a body planet. The estimated 60 billion body cells report every sensation back to the brain, the body's thinking centre, in which experiences are sorted and classified. The whole body cooperates to react on each bit of information and every failure. Every emotion or successful bodily reaction is stored for future use. Laboratory rats have even helped to show scientists how they pass newly developed skills, trends and fears on to the babies of their next generation.

The information accumulated and stored in physical cells is recycled by Earth after a body dies, but I transfer the thought memories from human minds to their collective consciousness.

Another task that I have is to return some of the available information from the collective human consciousness to people who meditate. Yes, information can indeed return from the collective human consciousness to those individuals who seek new and ancient wisdom in states of receptivity. However, only a limited number of humans are able to tune into the whole of consciousness, to which all minds are linked.

This useful tool (of meditation) is available to everyone, but misunderstood by some as an open door to demonic possession. Contrary to prayers, which allow personal thought streams to dictate personal needs, meditation is just a simple way to balance the frequency waves of human brains for optimal awareness of the available information out there.

As with many earthly rituals, meditation can become an addictive habit for those who prefer to withdraw from the physical world and remain in a state of bliss.

Only a few humans, like Nikola Tesla, Einstein, Edgar Cayce and Nostradamus, for example, have been able to tap into this information network by either quieting their own thoughts or focusing on creative thoughts.

Humans have furthermore found another way to access the information within the collective human consciousness by using chemical substances.

Which leaves us with the rest of humanity, who seldom strive to think beyond existing ideas, preferring to remain stagnant in their own comfort zones.

It is those who are willing to think that I am interested in. Those with the ability to recycle existing information and come up with extraordinary, mind-blowing mental creations to help move and change human consciousness.

So the next time when lightning deprives your swimming pool of chlorine, you may understand that electricity also collects information from the water in your body.

Whenever your body reacts by producing goose-bumps at the noise of thunder, you will remember it is only me hitting on one of the Earth's neurons to transfer your and your loved ones' memories to the collective human brain.

An Ode to Energy

Goddess, how beautiful you are in that glorious white dress. How subtly you hide your weakness behind the pure white light. How many stars will you devour at every change of your attire? How uncontrollably DNA serves your power! Who will quench your constant lust? Since you cannot be destroyed, how is it that your glitter fades if not constantly fed? Who ignited the stream that burns from your heart? Who controls the force that is and always was – your ever-present moving life?

**Defining Everything: A Theory of All
by The Author**

ENERGY
A hundred years before Einstein, the French scientist Antoine Lavoisier proved that "things" can transform into "nothing". His experiment showed that in any transformation not a single amount of matter is ever lost and neither is any amount of matter ever gained. He heated up a measured volume of water, ran the steam that formed through an iron pipe and then cooled it back into water. The quantity of water regained was less than the quantity that was originally boiled. However, when the mass of the regained water plus the steam that had been left inside as well as a mass increase to the iron pipe were summed up they amounted to the exact mass of the water before it was boiled.

If we begin to see "things" and "nothings" as part of, and never apart from each other, we may understand that they form a single whole, a single continuum of energy that includes all of existence. Einstein's famous $E=MC^2$ proves that energy can become mass and mass can become energy, that the two are not separate but interlinked as one. This continuum comprises energy in its myriad physical as well as invisible forms.

If matter and space form the continuum of energy, it implies that "things" do not *have* energy, but rather *are* energy; thus reducing the whole of existence to be compiled only of energy. And for energy to take on a myriad different forms along the continuum of "all and none" – motion is the key. Without motion "nothing" cannot gather into "things" and "things" cannot split into "nothing".

MOTION
Every form of energy in this continuum of everything moves as a unique frequency. It wasn't that long ago when science discovered that all forms of matter are frequency waves (Stephen Hawking, *The Grand Design*). This revelation suggests that matter does not *have* motion inside as was previously believed, but rather, that matter *is* frequency waves. Long before this discovery, it was already known that things such as light, sound and space are frequency waves. This proves that everything in the continuum of energy (matter and space) *is* in fact motion. Motion causes this single energy to change into the variety of "things" and "nothings" that make up the universe.

If energy is motion, it means that motion always was and always will be, because in the absence of motion there can only be complete and utter stagnation. Without motion time cannot be, because motion causes all the rhythms and cycles of existence. Neither would there be the resulting sounds, colours, shapes, fragrances, flavours, temperatures not even life itself. Energy is separated only by the difference in its frequencies, which also provides the different energies with unique characteristics.

Separated frequencies combine to form new ones. Our bodies are wonderful examples of different energy frequencies that have combined to form a unique unit of "matter and space" vibrating at a specific frequency. The human body is made up of many frequencies scaling from slow, up to super-fast ones: for example, bones (slow), flesh (faster), blood (faster), air (even faster) and electricity (the fastest).

It is inside this combination of slow- and fast-moving energy frequencies that life is found; life, which can be defined as the ability to move about independently and create new motion frequencies at will. However, life is only possible with the exact and correct combination of energy frequencies combined in a separate unit. If one of the energy frequencies changes, the remaining frequencies will start to move apart. When this happens, the body as a living unit will cease to exist. The energy frequencies will also separate from each other in a specific sequence, from fast to slow. Electricity will withdraw first, after that air, then flesh and blood, leaving just the bones.

Science has furthermore proved that energy cannot be created or destroyed but merely changes from one form to another (as previously mentioned). The conception and death of a human body is therefore a beautiful example of how energy frequencies change from one form to the next. Our flesh-blood-and-bone frequencies combine with those of earthly elements and transform as the body decomposes. Our breath-and-neuron frequencies dissolve into space where they are stored as memories. Nothing is ever lost in the continuum of all.

During a lifetime, our energy frequencies also combine with and change other frequencies in many ways. We combine with the energy frequencies of food (plants / animals), air and water to increase our own physical frequency, as our bodies change them into other forms. We also combine our frequencies with those of other human beings when we touch.

Our bodies can exist only within a certain range of energy frequencies. Energy frequencies that move too slowly or too fast compared with our own will also change their form. For example, severe cold will solidify and excessive heat will consume our bodies.

CHANGE
What is true of energy also relates to frequency because energy is frequency. Therefore if energy cannot be created or destroyed but just changes from one form to another, it can also be said that the energy of the continuum has never been created and can never be destroyed but that it has been and will always be moving through eternal cycles of change.

Change is inevitable in the face of motion; and change cannot take place without motion. We all know that when or wherever energy frequencies meet they will react on each other. They will change. They may synchronize to form symmetrical structures, duplicate like cells or collide and explode into a trillion pieces.

What else can cause motion and change but the attraction and repulsion between different energy frequencies? Chemistry explains that it has to do with the reaction to attraction and repulsion between combinations of different elements. Physics explains that electricity results when the fast frequency of electrons comes into contact with the slower frequency of matter (a conductor). Science says it is magnetism that happens when certain metals come into contact with each other. Cosmologists believe that the mystery of gravitational attraction lies within the property of "things" having mass. Nuclear science has it that energy is released when a proton enters the frequency of a neutron, splitting it up. Biology claims it is natural instinct, this physical attraction or repulsion between two bodies. And we think it is love when there is an additional attraction between the vibrations of two minds. There is no dispute that motion is written in the mechanics of the universe.

INFORMATION

It is the differences between energy frequencies that ultimately move them to attract or repel, causing change. It is the many different energy frequencies that fill the universe with unique information bits like shapes, colours, textures, fragrances, sounds and tastes.

When dissimilar energy frequencies combine or divide, information gains complexity. Yellow and blue become green; four triangles and a square become a pyramid; fragrances become perfume; and different sounds become language or music.

Information is therefore not separate from the continuum of energy frequencies but is what creates infinite motion and change. Since information is as much energy as motion, together the three form a trinity.

Information is an intrinsic part of the energy frequency trinity, and just like energy and frequency, information can also not be created or destroyed; it can only be recycled from one form to another. That means that every information energy frequency that was ever changed by means of our words, thoughts or deeds will forever exist, unless it is changed into a stronger or weaker one.

CONSCIOUSNESS
But what would all the shapes, colours, sounds, fragrances and tastes be without someone or something to experience and react to them? An awareness with volition and the capability to move itself and other objects around independently.

Unfortunately, our human bodies can detect only a very tiny portion of the information available in the continuum of information energy frequencies and our minds can comprehend even less. We are but specks of awareness within this whole of consciousness. We are a combination of the three. We are energy, we are motion and we are information. We are consciousnesses, with the sole purpose of vibrating at our true frequency, which can be found only within the layers between our passions and highest excitement.

The End
No, The Continuum

Seasons, Cycles and Time

The Life of a Flower

The tension before the bud bursts,
Then, effortless, the glory;
an antithesis of the unseen,
from admiration detached.

When Zephyr reminds, "All forms are fleeting",
the first petal drops from resistance.

Cut Flowers

Yesterday,
a blade separated the bunch
like umbilical cords
less the blood.

Now,
energy gathers light from the sun,
pins the blame on draining life and water,
which keeps the stems erect a few days less
than those of their rooted friends.

A Place to Overnight

To muzzle a day's singing,
every bird needs a safety net,
a dream catcher,
camouflage against a night,
a place to imbue itself as the ovary of a willing flower.

Birdsong

Silent anticipation precedes the show;

By the prologue of light, excitement breaks;
Some sing a single note, others a well known...

Between polyphony rises an intelligent tune
And a hundred promises that the sun will be soon.

**The Evolution of Wings
(with an apology to Darwin)**

Then winter came;
Bird-wings plumed into bat-wings;
moulting them into butterfly wings
for spring.

Eons ago they had fins to swim,
But they wanted to fly;
With every jump they feathered their scales
until they could.

Nowadays angels pilot UFOs;
Beetles raise their vibrational tones;
And whales drown in their efforts to crawl.

Nuptial Wings

Flying-ant rain strings them out (on a first and final flight),
Sets lamp-posts alive with whispering silk that hushes to heaps on the ground.

Flying-ant rain strings them out,
Beds their blind orgy
before they offer themselves to un-hatched eggs;
a purposeful life in less than an hour.

Timeless Growth

Heat serves moist from the sky.
Today, yesterday and tomorrow,
in my Hong Kong garden,
Fan palm flips fresh hands
and Frangipani yellow-eyes
Rubber tree rooting the sand.

Today, yesterday and tomorrow,
Lily will float in a petalled boat
in my Thailand garden; Heliconia will surrender,
and Elephant Ear will hear the wind de-pear
a tree.

Today, tomorrow and yesterday,
shadows sliced Delicious Monsters
in my Kwa-Zululand[2] garden, Creepers crept the dark,
Yuccas pierced the night
and Flamboyant shook blood from her palms.

Yesterday, Azalea creased white napkins;
Tomorrow, Strelitzia will file orange nails.

Yesterday and tomorrow
do not fertilize Asian gardens;
where all the plants grow today
(as their grammar does).

---

[2] Kwa-Zululand: South Africa.

They Change My Mind

On the day when impregnated islands give birth to our filth and plastic has become an element ...
I will mutate from a vegetarian into a vampire.

When Fukushima's sneeze infects the whole world and dolphins visit the coasts of Japan still ...
I'll refuse to believe in their intelligence.

When white rhinos mutate to be born hornless and oil-wrists are still being slit ...
I'll reincarnate in another universe.

Awareness Has Eyes

On mornings like this,
when paws and wings disturb the greenery…

Afternoons like this when a sunset occupies the cosmos…

Nights like these when meteorites
are no distraction from the stars…

It is, in moments like these,
when 'the theory of all' is lost…

in the split it is found.

Winter and Its Friends

I woke up to find them in my bed –
darkness scrambling eggs for a slumbering sun.

All along the equator nobody owns jerseys or needs
comforters.

They never see trees chameleon or sample the flavours
of cold.

Space, Place and Matter

The Midlands of Kwa-Zulu Natal (South Africa)

Thunderclouds dream up a storm,
A storm across KZN's curvaceousness.

Hatch-huts goose-bump her thousand hills,
Cling to her back like grey monkey babies.

Her armpits are burned to the roots;
Lush bush kaross[3] and cattle trail her valleys.

Her clay crafts;
Her fires cook;
(They cook every day life.)

Her smoke signals,
Signals secret lovers sharpening assegais[4] in the sparks,
Sun-sparks of their skilful replies.

---

[3] Kaross – a blanket made from animal skin.
[4] Assegai – a traditional Zulu weapon.

Zones of Comfort

Another town ferments among vineyards,
A church tower pistils the plain,
Winter soot pollens chimney-pots and trees drip an afternoon shower.

Another village sprouts from mossed stilts,
Weeds breathe vitally,
Pot plants green windowsills and bonsais sip the sea spray.

In both these towns,
Six jetlag hours apart,
Life burgeons as everywhere
but is seldom transplanted.

Familiar soils fertilize out-bloomed bulbs best.

Tell Me about the Hard Problems

The nothing hidden in everything,
The impossible quest for big, like the one for small,
Whether space and matter is a continuum.

Describe to me the density in diamonds,
The formula that transmutes elements into stars,

How do neutrinos fall through planets?

Direct me to a beginning or an ending
at the top or bottom of the world.

Teach me how cosmic clocks click in different
dimensions,
How thoughts filtrate in the layers between time zones.

Share with me the everything in nothing,
The number of heartbeats
conscious motion wishes to grant.

Space – Ever Growing in a Confined Unit?

Could the slow problem with mountains be that their growth is inhibited by the extent to which space is willing to expand?
Consider unfolding leaves displacing the air sooner than the dying ones,
Falling drops that drive winds faster than sands can sink water and births that fill available space faster than the time decomposition takes.
Not to mention the different rates at which stardust clumps and supernovas explode.
Is space confined, inflated, or infinite?

Thought Theories

Everything always is:
As bubbles in beer appear in thousands out of one...
The way they push up against gravity and ice,
weighing less than water,
breaks natural laws.

Everything always moves...
Like electrons network roots,
Lungs divide air,
Blood vessels tube,
Lighting-bolts fork,
Rivers carve grooves,
The way they branch and split fingers to point at the
unified field of this everything.

Of the Surreal and the Spiritual

Life Lives Me

I once was something else – a volcano, a seeder and a giraffe.
This time I'm a blinking, pulsating machine energized by sensory stimuli.

I once did something else – crawled, slithered and spun,
But now I circulate blood and edit dreams.

I once was somewhere else – in lightning, caves and cocoons.
For nine months I lived without lungs,
Now micro-lives live in my cells.

From This World and in It

I didn't buy any of the world's rivers
they all belong to me.
As soon as I wake up in a dream,
I open my mouth and the jungle rains in.

The one,
In whose ears ferns unfurl,
Whose lashes dangle like aerial roots,
Whose pores osmose spores,
I, wilted by maggots and funguses,
Lie separated from nature unexposed in my clothes.

The Stretch Between Sleep and Awakening: Dormiveglia

6 am – Synesthesia:
Reality alarms at the door of my dreams,
From the thin layer between consciousnesses
I emerge to see the orgasm of sound,
a liquid rainbow.

12 noon – Perception:
My senses feed on information and my brain patiently digests
300 000 billion inputs per second but I never heard the music that auroras make.

11.30 pm – Unconsciousness:
The other realm unlocks my imagination to look at stored information from various bizarre angles

High Rises

Here, where a sun confuses shadows,
The movement of pot plants speaks of something more
than just paving and buildings
And the human quest is for comfort.

Somewhere, where winds dune rocks,
It will be easier to think of you as a combination of
elements about to change form,
Where life not death is the mystery and the quest for
comfort is human.

There, where planets share the sky,
I will hide behind the moon's broken side,
The side that landed fourth on the missing list of the
human quest for comfort.

Dharma

To enter please exit and to delete please repeat.

The texture of his book is a peach,
It's not his skin,
It feels like his being;
The manner in which he sits,
A quiet mountain under mist.
His smile fills eyes with alkaline milk.
I trip over his voice and land on wisdom.

To exit please enter and to repeat please delete.

Three Wise Men

Their words: rivalled, ridiculed, misunderstood.
Their awareness: *Dukkha*, *maya* and sin.
Their offers: enlightenment, salvation, non-suffering.
Their theories: far ahead of their times.
Their directions: three pointing at one.
Our choice: to remain stuck.

Reincarnation

When the son of God was born the first few times,
He had other names,
He was murderers and rapists.
During the next few lives he recalled the senselessness,
Then became rulers –
Ordering his servants to kill the disobedient.

Two thousand years ago,
He was born evolved
And they called him Jesus,
Who aspired to tell the rest of the world:
"I am God,
Gold and silver mean nothing,
Take my things,
Take my life,
All that matters is our love."

His disciples wanted to know whether he was Elijah
Or maybe John the Baptist,
But he smiled,
Said: make up your own minds.

Then the unaware nailed him like a worldly attachment,
And as promised he did return because they didn't understand the first time when he explained that we are one.

The Tai Chi Dancer

His face: a blink-less emptiness,
Hands unglue the air that sticks to them,
Like adding to and ridding from his aura.

Legs balance the erect male frame,
Fingers rotate as if spinning chakras,
Spine hinges a hundred-and-eighty-degree bow and off he goes.

The man knows something that I don't.

Eastern Wisdom

Laozi, who whispered the Dao De Jing?

And how is nature treating the Gobi?

Laozi, please watch out,
Capitalism and his concrete army are approaching fast.

They're plotting to kill Nature as well as her balance.

Thalamus
(with an apology to Proust)

Expressions of Consciousness

All the sweetness and sap stored in a melon pip,
All the redness runs red,
The greenness grows green.
I close my eyes…

Listen to the foghorn's warning,
Feel the breeze rubbing my cheeks,
Can it already be the Magnolia tree?
I open my eyes…

All the blackness and sparks from one fallen night.

Rasasvada

My thoughts are running taps,
While they should be soaking like this body in a tub,
Enjoying the pleasure of bubbles bursting on wet skin,
The qualia of heat and how the temperature s-l-o-w-l-y drops,
The conscious indulgence,
The caution not to ripple the surface.

Feel (1)

The word for it is body –
This sensory thing…

Maybe it's not a sin –
This nippling…

Maybe it's not forbidden –
This quivering…

Maybe we may enjoy –
This engulfing of fibre known as skin,
This trembling…
Tactiling under the fingers and tongue of water and wind's –
Luring.

Feel (2)

Daybreak: afloat in the pool,

Sun on my face,

When out of the blue: the rain.

Equation for a Retina

Choose a single star;
Imagine a line that joins it to your eye;
Measure the distance from here to there;
Compare the speed of sight to that of light;
Multiply the possibilities rendered by space;
Divide them by the echoes from a long-dead sun.

The Sound of Sight

Backpacked, we conquered the Peak.
Our silhouettes edged by dusk,
Wrapped in a wilderness,
Captured by a rawness,
Disturbed to awareness,
Defeated – we paused.

The Other Sides of Silence

Listen to this species make love and rape,
Hear them cage birds and free murderers,
Ignore the famine-grunts from their abundant world,
Ear witness them pay to poach and beg to save,
Entertain them with scores of violence and grace,
Soundproof their orphanages and old-age homes,
Now, listen…

They managed to create something beautiful…
Can you hear them music?

Hear the Bigger Picture

Was our separation voluntary?
Hence the fear of isolation,
The desperation for reattachment...

I hear a group of children sing and for a moment
experience the whole being pulled back together.

When My Senses Become Extinct

When my mind and I abandon this body and its ears,
We won't be able to hear what goes on around here.

In that in-between dreamlike state,
We will move among trees dependent on bird echoes.
We will lie down on river banks and imagine frogs,
insects and beetles.

We'll dance in golden circles, oblivious to the latest
songs being performed,
as we sing along to those we knew from before.

We'll be blown away by the images we recall,
as we walk across wetlands and plains,
move through mountains and walls,
without any feet or eyes.

My mind and I will smell and taste the roasts
being served at familiar dinner-tables,
with remembered tongues and noses.

We won't have fingers to touch our loved ones' skins
but we'll connect to their frequencies
and chat to their reminiscences.

When my mind and I abandon this body,
We'll be angry about the times we spent online;
On writing poetry;
We'll regret the lack of sensations and experiences,
that we could have used
to recycle the information of eternity.

Creators and Their Art

"To create one's own world takes courage."
– Georgia O'Keeffe

All Humans Are Artists

A metaphysical force moves as atoms.
It imbues bodies at conception
and shares the qualia in experiences.

A curious force moves in the senses.
It portions its consciousness with humanity.

An expressive force directs thoughts
into audios, narrates autobiographies,
salvages memories into fictional fantasies,
synchronizes body-sounds with musical instruments,
and remixes the order of sentences into poetics.

It's an artisan.
It wings ideas to become detectable.
It makes symbolic illustrations out of imaginations:
demonstrations of light, line and shape;
recreations of creation and two- and three-D
thought-presentations.

It's an active force that simulates feelings,
turning them into acts, mimes and dances.

This insensible force nourishes intuitions
to blend ingredients into recipes;
and combine concentrates into perfumes.

The life force haunts free-wills to share inscapes.
It inspires intelligences to transform natural into
artificial worlds.
It structures the chaos of landscapes;
adds interest with sculptures and installations.

It turns beehives and ammonite-shells
into irrefutable
numbers.

Super Consciousness

Like a dream trapped in a statue…
an experiment becomes this experience.

Like the rhythm of juice in a branch…
the wind razors sound.

As light bends to penetrate a prism…
memory stores blood.

While decomposition foams the ground,
the male-female dual-personality
turns its talents into us.

Star Quality
(Inspired by Roland Barthes, 1915-1980)

Cheers to the modifiers of thoughts –
The unintentional changers of minds –
The creators of works
destined to revolt or stun!

To those,
who touch with words like fingertips,
refusing to pastiche or duplicate.

The catalyzers –
disturbers of the mundane –
who, by ordinary things,
cast hypnotic spells.

Here is to the women and men
who help to find the unfathomable
in the gaps between perception
and the melds of brush-strokes or sounds!

Sex in Oils

Watch transparent colours
flow around each other,
over each other,
with each other
into marble.

See how warm shades glow,
how dark ones shadow,
how white lifts light,
how pigments entwine,
blend with, and enter each other
into mud.

Can That Be Art?

A pair of used gloves hung in a corridor. –

Must be important to someone.

They're irrelevant
to most.

They can be a glimpse of a life
to some.

To others:
the ordinary by awareness revealed –

Just like art:
in which nothing is.

Commissions

And then...
Times are spent
on decorating homes
in beautiful,
colour-coordinated,
skilfully executed,
thoughtless,
masterpieced copies
of existence.

"The holy grail is to spend less time making the picture than it takes people to look at it." – Banksy

Conceptual Works

That which is painted introduces
a language
foreign to a brain,
yet renowned to a mind.

This painted
differs from one's blood
in shade,
but not in taste.

It recognizes one from womb water.

It takes one's feet for mud-pool cleaving;

gathers inner-smiles like small change.

It invites one in to be with it.

One won't need eyes
to hear of meaning,
but hands to lead one (all arms)

away from it.

Art Therapy

Illustrate your illusions,
Write your therapist a poem,
Paint your own still life,
Shoot the streets where you roam.

Sculpt a twisted thought,
Fake a true biography,
Decorate a bitter cake,
Sew your troubles in a tapestry.

Befriend them with who is who,
Sell them at a steal,
Exhibit them on a lawn,
or market them as surreal.

"The position of the artist is humble. The artist is essentially a channel." – Piet Mondrian

Déjà Vu

A book will find readers
to share life experiences
among a million others
they already had
as pupas, mushrooms and spiders –

inexplicable recognitions,
yet deeply understood
by the music in the sentences –

resolute for more reminders….

Rocks also found painters
to conserve human shapes
among a million others
they already had
as crystals, mermaids and viruses.

Inexplicable forms,
Yet deeply understood
from Duende's dances –

resolute never to die out.

Where the Artists Are

Empty after a million-dollar taking: [like selling a child]
Entertained by a crowd of thoughts: [at a reception speech]
Admiring narcissists: [for social skills]
Balancing ego with doubt: [never ending]
Twisting thoughts: [the familiar ones]
Accepting fragments of life: [the expected ones]

Head-banging the rest. [Don't we all?]

Selling Us the Love Art Village (Nai Hang, in Thailand) in Perfect Broken English

"We all artists," he says.

"Just look, your beaded dress …

"See:
My inspiration from the clouds…
My friend from washed up coconuts…
This guy he make collages
but the rest of Thailand make copy art.

"First Sunday of the month
we play music and puppet show for kids."

But it was their paintings –
Every corner of their living-space –
that convinced: they live art.

And the quote by Brian Andreas framed to a wall:
"She said she usually cries at least once a day,
Not because she is sad
But because the world is so beautiful
And life is so short."

Local Colour

The universal language of movement
speaks in many tones.

Its crimson frequencies
(sometimes)
exceed a body's capacity
but they call it A-D-D[5].

The universal language of movement
turns the heat in healing hands
into shades of teal.

It tunes amber
into a psychic's broadband
and vibrates ochre
through horse-whisperer's eyes.

Mauve is the colour
of this universal language,
pulsating through space
at an azure pace.

And topaz –
the shade of forgotten rain dances –

Remember topaz?

---

[5] A-D-D: Attention Deficit Disorder.

Science in the Arts

The symphony of quantum and string
by Weber and Mozart;

The architecture of heaven and hell
by da Vinci and Van Gogh;

The erotica in non- and fiction
by Einstein and Neruda;

The vibrato of rhythm in sound
by Mercury and Muskrat;

Each reveals the "theory of all"
that Hawking is searching for.

Tate Modern (London, UK, August 2011)

"Oh please, if I have to face another soup can!

Well I never...
At last,
something different!

...artifact or artishit?

Thank God it's not in four-D.

Maybe from a different angle
the meaning will unfold:

Form?
Irony?
Melancholy?
Metaphor?

It's right here on the tip of my tongue...

Nope, should rather have opted for the guided tour."

Interpreting Nature's Art

The day lessens.

A battered face drags
a torch across the night.

It sketches zebras on jail floors.

It's a rabbit!

No, it's a sea-nipped,
chubby-cheek smile.

It's a balloon floating in wine.

No, it's nature's copy art.

Maybe it's a way for the Messiah to be seen…

in a million reflections
of one light.

Cancri e (Super Earth)

Have you ever flown
(without wings)
to the constellation of Cancer in a dream?

… for an exhibition of a planet: double the size of the earth,
where a year lasts eighteen hours
and temperatures
top three-thousand nine hundred, degrees F?

Did you also stumble over astral rocks
and awake from a conscious shock?

Were you not blinded by the effulgence
constructed of this flawless diamond?

"It took me four years to paint like Raphael and a lifetime to paint like a child." – Pablo Picasso

Directions to the Fourth Dimension:

The children say:
There's this secret slipway.

Point they:
It's in the right brain.

Swear they:
Through there, consciousness escapes.

They insist:
One can dive into visions
that are begging to be materialized.

They promise:
There's an ocean of spoken words.

They whisper:
It's there that Fantasy hands her stories out.

I Want to Be What I Am Not

breathe in the deep as if with gills;

jump off a cliff as if with wings;

like angels, navigate the Milky Way;

like lightning, fire forests;

pray in tongues like Christians;

speak to the dead like psychics;

levitate like Sufis;
detach like Buddhists;

paint like…
speak like…
and write like…
everybody but myself.

Mentors Suggest

Explain and the magic is lost.

Make the concrete cry.

Teach it how to walk.

(Snip and tuck.)

Show the concrete's blood.

Let readers decide for themselves
and at the end, slap them blind.

The Poem I Cannot Yet Write

One day I will write a poem.

My tongue will no longer be a fish on a hook;
my hands will no longer be crabs with tied-up legs;
my language won't be transparent jellyfish;
and my emotions will be a full-grown whale.

On that day,

I will write a poem
rich and alive like the sea,
a poem made from ebbs- and-flows.

I will make it trace all the coral's curves
and give it texture like mother-of-pearl.

This poem will ocean the entire world

because it will hold in it

my children.

On Relationships, Life and Death

Sarang (I wish to be with you until death)

I didn't fall for your eyes,
trip over your wit or drown in your smiles.

It wasn't the jeans you wore or how they wore you,
it was the mirror in which I saw us.

"Out beyond ideas of wrongdoing and rightdoing, there is a field. I'll meet you there." – Rumi

The Field

And in that field –
not a blade of guilt;

Nobody –
but yours and mine.

Only unarmed moments spent in arms,
and whenever we leave that field…
it disappears.

You Said You Had a Dream

You said you never had such thoughts before.

You said suddenly you saw,
But you didn't say what…

You suspended your upper arm
too long against mine,

I said, that's what dreams are for –
our fears and desires.

You said, let's not
talk about it anymore.

After I Dropped You off at the Airport

Three days swept together…

About eighteen of my long, lost hairs;
Four of yours;
A price tag;
A few biscuit-crumbs;
and a hundred
grains of sea sand.

Three day's dust
dance through a room
to the tune of sunbeams,
by a lonely broom.

Self Talk

I've never noticed a difference
in the flavour of toothpaste,
with the previous one still fresh on my tongue;

How promises should last
as long as it takes for a plastic tube
to disintegrate.

A patient room never asks for a return-date,
And so much has changed over the years
apart from the faces on this photograph.

Tomorrow,
I will replace this pillowcase;
After that,
I won't, ever again,
watch the clock practice ballet.

Expatriates

Fears festered from the core,
Trickled to a near-explosion,
and we lived (as if normally)
along with that,
for far too long.

But who could have predicted
the highs and lows
that were about to unfold?
How easy it would be to plan ahead,
and difficult to let go.

And how could we have known
something within would outgrow the need
for a typhoon to spiral us home?

**Then Strangers Met
(the birth of a child)**

The faceless relationship lasted for months,
as if we found each other online.

I grew fond of it being like that.

The meeting was complicated.

You came bloodied and soaked,
I felt exposed
and bewildered when your eyes
opened your doubt.
(No, *be-wondered* –
that's what I was
in the role of your mum.)

So I flannelled you in,
Asked approval of my milk,
Introduced your cries to my skies,
Lifted your nose
to the fragrances drawn
from the dirt
by an African storm.

A True Story, 1954

Born at a full moon's blink,
A six-pounder in orange
curls is taken away to be bathed.

Upon return, fixed
to a bulging breast.

They're all born with two eyes,
Ten fingers and ten toes…

"All is well with this one," says Mrs Roodt,
blankets him and rings the bell.

"Nurse, this is not my child."

The nurse reads the nametag
with a smug, "See here!
It's clearly written, 'Jannie Roodt'."

"Miss, please,
there should be another ginger,
birth-marked on the upper right chest:
that one is my son."

The Girl We Called Mum

She adorned the room with sunshine to disturb our morning sleep;
Pinched snapdragon jaws during our midday reveries;
Culled comets in her apron, to kindle our dreams.

The only one, who knew if motherhood came naturally,
was she.

Childhood *versus* Adulthood

A stagnant nucleus on a playground,
surrounded by electrons,
expressing themselves as motion –
cavorting, tripping and laughing out
loudly.

To them the nucleus
doesn't exist (at this moment).

Imagine the nucleus expressing herself as motion…
allowing life exuberantly to flow from her core,
to run, fall and hide just like them;

Applying self-control only when
reminded of her role.

**Inspired by a Note Little Fin Wrote to Her Mum
"You're so beautiful I could cry."**

Just like I could cry
for the little people of this world
because they are so beautiful.

I could cry for this one
with a button missing
from a hand-me-down shirt;
that one, whose permanent
teeth grew skew;
Those who bring money for lunch,
and those who bring none.

I could cry for them –
getting into trouble
because no one has checked
if homework was done;

those who are told, "Speak up,
look at me when I talk
to you, and it's none
of your business."

I could cry for the stupid
who are clever
enough to know that they are;

the naughty one with psoriasis
drying his fingers out.

I cry over porcelain dolls
dropped by teachers;
the middle child;
the eldest who made space for the others;
the one over-shadowed by a brother.

Some laugh at kids
who are afraid of Santa
or devastated by the lie;
but I cry for them too.

I cry
for the gum-sniffers;
the outsiders, those degraded by skin tones
or slow metabolisms.

I cry for little shoulders
slumped under school bags.

Like a child, I cry
over small dreams that
don't count in a parent's eyes;

the crushed, that handed in their sparks.

And Fin, I could cry
when your muse speaks
so beautifully.

From your grade one teacher.

A Better Life

Suspended clouds,
grey-white and pinked into candy floss,
hang fluffed across the sky after yesterday's storm.

A child and her baby brother,
Eased to sleep by the surface
of a wooden plank.

– One cannot dream of comfort
without memories.–

A hill, textured by shades of green,
reflects last night's dew-gathering
against a grey building.

"My name is Mabel," smiles,
(when no-one sees).
Is, "Fine, thank you"
(with all that she knows).

School-bagged and uniformed,
like all the other girls;
English-coursed (for free),
during (what should have been)
summer playtimes for six year olds.

The world rotates,
beautifully balanced by abundance.
It is her world too.

But this she will only realize
once she grasps the purpose of two English words:

red and tape.

Grounded

By The Hong Kong children:

In summer, we will only remove our shoes
at beaches, swimming pools, or the front doors of
homes.

For the rest of the year, our feet will experience
the impact against concrete, at various levels,
as we step over cracks and jump joints.

They will be safely wrapped in the latest autumn,
winter or spring collections; iced over with leather
flowers; tied up with neon laces; or plat-formed
by squeaky soles and/or flickering lights.

But you will never see us bare the authentic pair,
for that's considered impolite.

By The South African children:

In summer, it is a rule to come to school
without shoes.

We can feel hollows under hardened
and fragile curls of peeling mud.

We can dip sleepy feet into morning grass,
crumb them with dry sand,
Then wipe patches from them against bark,
clambering past cautious friends,
clinging hard to sturdy branches,
to join the daring ones up higher,
at the cost of a cracked arm or a leg-bone
(for some more than twice).

When our running flattens autumn leaves,
We don't dread winter's coming
as much as the thought of our feet
deprived of nature's touch,
the thought of them growing
soft in shoes, in the months to come.

In a Tree House

Those were the days when it felt
safe to be surrounded by black widows,
waiting in their webs
to venom their partners
after sex.

Retro was the soft cherry cakes.

Most tastes were nude as caramel,
and my mind…
how it played and played
with tiger-tails.

"I want to be with those who know secret things or else alone." – Rainer Maria Rilke

A Biography

Hang a purpose on me   not jewelry.
Foster my needs   forget the wants.
I'd rather go nude   than superficially dressed.
Prefer opposition   to false flattering.
Choose to be ignored   rather than gibbered at.
Surprise and shock me or else stay home.

Noises from the Apartment Above (Hong Kong)

Footsteps run a bath.

It can only be a woman,
echoing a series of directionless
paths across a few square feet
at such a nervous beat,
much too early,
much too fast.

Her front door slams.

A silent relief
carpets the floor above in a quiet rug
till dusk, when the next
leg of her frenzy will start.

I wonder where she spends
the rest of her days, gathering
energy to steal away
my sanity?

C-Ward Positivity

"Spare your energy for a laugh.
OK, a smile will do.

Do you realize how lucky you are? –

I mean that thing about a better place. –

And please, when you get there, say hello for us!

Maybe you can cheat God out of this pain.
Just tell Him that you lost it on this side.
We will try to hide it as well as we can;
And, if you can get away with that,
He may consider casting you
in the supporting role
next time."

The Night She Passed

He disposes of a banana peel;	useless.
Catches the night bus:	last passenger.
Notices a starless sky	with barely a moon.
Enters the apartment's	darkness.
Adds shampoo to a non-existing	shopping list.
Listens to an unplugged TV's	silence.
The fridge offers	coldness.
He lines up to enter	sleeplessness.
Dreams of a hospital bed's	emptiness.
where a laundry basket	
holds on to	her fragrance.

Mind *versus* Brain

My sister had a stroke.

It was nothing like stroking a cat...
more like
a stroke of bad luck.

Estimated, that it
(the stroke)
twisted half her mind,
then pinched it off with a clot
and now the left-over half
confuses her brain with voided concepts;
Hence, she speaks like a poet.

People live normal lives
with under-developed brains;
Even cope with pieces cut away.

Cells are supposed to renew themselves,
And the fibres of hers are intact, but
her mind is trapped –
a balloon in a door,
half-way in and half-way out –
It should have burst, but it never did.

Sometimes babies are born like this –
with minds halfway in and halfway out.

And some of us age like rusting pipes,
from which memories leak,
drop by drop.

Other minds leave in a single pop.

Epilogue

The creations of minds are removed from reality.
They build emotional attachments,
romanticise,
Add music and new settings
to live in,

But it's the knowing
that oozes:

A knowing in disguise,
Impossible to define,
yet very bright at times.

A knowing, that I am not…
Who I want to be,
Where I want to be,
With all whom I want to be

The knowing, that somewhere
life is happening and I…
I have missed out.

The knowing, that good times
are glimpses into happiness,

It's memories we live off
And that's why blue skies hurt.

The End
No, The Continuum

Bibliography and Sources

I wish to acknowledge the following authors and their works from which I have drawn the inspiration to write my own philosophical meditations:

Susan J. Blackmore, Dr, *Consciousness: An Introduction*, New York, USA, Oxford University Press, 2004.

Gregg Braden, *Spontaneous Healing of Belief*, London, UK, Hay House, 2008.

Will Buckingham, Douglass Burnham, Clive Hill, Peter J. King, John Marenbon, Marcus Weeks, Richard Osborne, Stephanie Chilman, *The Philosophy Book*, London, Great Britain, Dorling Kindersley Ltd, (Penguin Group), 2011.

Jeremy Campbell, *Grammatical Man*, Suffolk, Great Britain, Penguin, 1984.

Julia Cameron, *The Artist's Way,* London, UK, Souvenir Press, 1994.

Catherine Collin, Nigel Benson, Joannah Ginsburg, Voula Grand, Merrin Lazyan, Marcus Weeks, *The Psychology Book*, London, UK, Dorling Kindersley Ltd, (Penguin Group), 2012.

Masaru Emoto, Translated into English from Japanese by T. T. David and A.Thayne, *The Hidden Messages in Water*, Hillsboro, Oregon, USA, Beyond Words Publishing, 2004.

Keith Flynn, *The Rhythm Method, Razzmatazz and Memory*, Blue Ash, Ohio, USA, Writers Digest Books, 2007.

Joshua Foer, *Moonwalking with Einstein*, London, UK, Penguin Books Ltd, 2011.

Stephen Hawking, *A Brief History of Time/ The Universe in a Nutshell*, New York, USA, Bantam Dell, 2001.

Stephen Hawking, *The Grand Design*, Great Britain, Transworld Publishers, 2010.

A.N. Hodge, *The History of Art*, London, UK, Arcturus Publishing Ltd, 2010.

Edward Hoffman, *The Wisdom of Carl Jung*, New York, USA, Kensington Publishing Corp., 2003.

Erik Hoffmann, *New Brain, New World*, London, UK, Hay House, 2012.

Lawrence M. Krauss, *A Universe from Nothing*, London, UK, Simon & Schuster, 2012.

J. Krishnamurti, *The First and Last Freedom*, New York, USA, Harper Collins, 1975.

Primo Levi, Translated into English from Italian by Raymond Rosenthal, *The Periodic Table*, London, UK, Penguin Classics, 2000.

Christopher Masters, *Dali*, London, UK, Phaidon Press Ltd, 1995.

Francois Mathey, *The Impressionists*, New York, USA, Frederick A. Praeger, Inc., Publishers, 1969.

Rebecca McClanahan, *Word Painting*, Cincinnati, Ohio, USA, Writers Digest Books, 1999.

Thelma Moss, Dr, *The Probability of the Impossible*, Los Angeles, USA, J. P. Tarcher, Inc., 1974.

Michael Newton, *Journey of Souls*, Woodbury, Minnesota, USA, Llewellyn Publications, 1994.

Yoko Ono, *Between the Sky and my Head*, Translated into English by Allison Plath-Moseley, Penelope Eifrig. Verlag der Buchhandlung Walther Konig, Koln, Germany, 2008.

Martin Plimmer and Brian King, *Beyond Coincidence*, New York, USA, St Martin's Press, 2007.

Carl Sagan, *Cosmos*, London, UK, Abacus, 1995.

Hans TenDam, *Exploring Reincarnation*, UK, Penguin, 1990.

Eckhart Tolle, *The New Earth*, London, England, Penguin, 2005.

Eckhart Tolle, *The Power of Now*, London, UK, Hodder and Stoughton Ltd, 2005.

Geoff Welch, *Humankind and the Cosmos*, New South Wales, Australia, Halbooks Avalon, 1999.

Johann von Wolfgang, *Goethe's Color Theory*, New York, UK, Van Nostrand Reinhold, 1971.

Advance Responses

Reading Celia Claase's debut collection *The Layers Between* has the sense of a journey stretching back to the meditations of the pre-Socratic philosophers then suddenly landing plumb in the midst of 20th century surrealism. It takes one back to a moment even before the Big Bang to a present where the future is ultimately unknowable yet at the same time as close to us as our own inner layers of skin. Her work is not esoteric or mystical though it certainly dwells in the realms of the metaphysical. However, the everyday 'ordinary' world of playgrounds, food, aprons and sex is never altogether absent. If the first part of the book contains philosophical narratives dealing with concepts such as space, time, motion and the elements, the second part consists of poems dealing with issues of the transient material world. As Claase perceptively states in one of the narratives: 'You experience me as metaphysical although I have the same characteristics as physical matter'.

Claase recognizes that the aspects of the physical world are 'nothing but combinations of the various energies moving at different frequencies, which ultimately determine their shapes and densities'. It is this understanding that allows us to slide easily into a Daliesque universe where 'We were in Saint Petersburg, which was not Saint Petersburg. We were assembling a wall but called it a table.'

In the poems we know that 'Awareness has eyes'. It is a world of Fukushima, dolphin hunts, poached rhinos and slit wrists. Whether in Thailand or in South Africa, there are clouds, hills, fires, circulating blood and edited dreams. We are the species that makes love and rapes. We free murderers and 'ignore the famine-grunts' from our 'abundant world'. But while the zones of comfort may be diminishing, Claase recognizes the interrelationship of the physical and metaphysical, the seen and the unseen. She perceives 'the fear of isolation/The desperation for reattachment' and is able to 'hear a group of children sing and for a moment/ experience the whole being pulled back together'. She has the ability to cut through the illusions of material gain, security and power: she may not have bought any of the world's rivers, but they all belong to her. As she wakes up in a dream 'I open my mouth and the jungles rain in'. *The Layers Between* is the recognition of 'as above, so below', and the joyous, yet calm, realization that samsara is nirvana and nirvana is samsara.

Gary Cummiskey
Johannesburg. July 2015

The Layers Between unfolds its philosophical conceits with a kind of artfully organic movement; flowing as it does between carefully wrought, playful monologues and compact, pithy poems. This collection is beautifully put together, the sequence of voices progressing with the kind of crystalline logic a reader might expect from natural, mythic and conceptual archetypes given voice and reflecting on what they perceive of the world. Conversely to expectation, it is the anthropomorphic monologues, designed to explore theories of being and believing, that demonstrate compassion and humanity; while the more intimate glimpses of the everyday shown in the poetry sections highlight a more clinical beauty and clarity of vision. The two sections work together admirably as a pathway for the reader's own ideas and formulations; an invitation to step into the world, and inhabit it with open eyes and minds.

Viki Holmes
author of *miss moon's class*

WRITE TO US!

We are interested to read **your** comments on
Celia Claase's,
The Layers Between.
Write to our email address,
proverse@netvigator.com,
giving us a few sentences
which you are willing for us to publish,
describing your response to this book.
If your comments are chosen to be included
in our E-Newsletter or website,
we will select another title published by Proverse
and send you a complimentary copy.
Please include your name, email address and mailing
address when you write to us, and state whether or not
we may cut or edit your comments for publication.
We will use your initials to attribute your comments.

ABOUT PROVERSE HONG KONG

Proverse Hong Kong (PVHK) is based in Hong Kong with long-term and expanding regional and international connections.

Proverse has published novels, novellas, non-fiction (including autobiography, biography, history, memoirs, sport, travel narratives, fictionalized autobiography), single-author poetry and short-story collections, children's, teens / young adult, educational and academic books.

Other interests include diaries, and academic works in the humanities, social sciences, cultural studies, linguistics and education.

Some Proverse books have accompanying audio texts. Some have been translated into Chinese. Others have been translated from other languages.

Proverse welcomes authors who have a story to tell, wisdom, perceptions or information to convey, a person they want to memorialize, a neglect they want to remedy, a record they want to correct, a strong interest that they want to share, skills they want to teach, and who consciously seek to make a contribution to society in an informative, interesting and well-written way. Proverse works with texts by non-native-speaker writers of English as well as by native English-speaking writers.

The name, "Proverse", combines the words "prose" and "verse" and is pronounced accordingly.

THE INTERNATIONAL PROVERSE PRIZE

The Proverse Prize, an annual international competition for an unpublished single-author book-length work of fiction, non-fiction, or poetry, was established in January 2008. It is open to all who are at least eighteen on the date they sign the entry form and without restriction of nationality, residence or citizenship.

The objectives of the prize are: to encourage excellence and / or excellence and usefulness in publishable written work in the English Language, which can, in varying degrees, "delight and instruct". Entries are invited from anywhere in the world.

The Prize
1) Publication by Proverse Hong Kong, with
2) Cash prize of HKD10,000 (HKD7.80 = approx. US$1.00)

Extent of the Manuscript: within the range of what is usual for the genre of the Entered Manuscript. However, the following indications may be useful: novel, short-story collection, non-fiction (e.g. autobiography, biography, diary, essay collection, journal, letters, memoir, etc.) -- 75,000 to 110,000 words; novella -- 30,000 to 50,000 words; poetry collection -- 5,000 to 25,000 words. Other word counts and mixed genre submissions are not ruled out.

KEY DATES FOR THE PROVERSE PRIZE IN ANY YEAR
(subject to confirmation and/or change)

Receipt of Entry Fees/ Forms	14 April to 31 May
Receipt of entered manuscripts	1 May to 30 June
Semi-finalists announced	July-September
Finalists announced	October-December
Winner(s) announced	March to November of the year that follows the year of entry
Winning book(s) published	Within the period, beginning in November of the year that follows the year of entry
Cash award made	At the same time as publication of the winning work(s)

More information, updated from time to time, is available on the Proverse Hong Kong website: <www.proversepublishing.com>.

The free Proverse E-Newsletter includes ongoing information about the Proverse Prize.
To be put on the free E-Newsletter mailing-list, email: <info@proversepublishing.com>
with your request.

**PROVERSE PRIZE WINNERS 2009-2014
ALREADY PUBLISHED
BY PROVERSE HONG KONG**

Rebecca Tomasis
Laura Solomon
Gillian Jones
David Diskin
Peter Gregoire
Sophronia Liu
Birgit Linder
James McCarthy
Philip Chatting
Celia Claase

POETRY PUBLISHED BY PROVERSE

If you have enjoyed Celia Claase's *The Layers Between*, you may also enjoy the following poetry collections / poetic works also published by Proverse.

Alphabet, by Andrew S. Guthrie. 2015.

Astra and Sebastian, by Lawrence Illsley. 2011.

Chasing Light, by Patricia Glinton Meicholas. 2013.

China Suite and other Poems, by Gillian Bickley. 2009.

For the Record and other Poems of Hong Kong, by Gillian Bickley. 2003.

Frida Kahlo's Cry and Other Poems, by Laura Solomon. 2015.

Heart to Heart: Poems, by Patty Ho. 2010.

Home, Away, Elsewhere, by Vaughan Rapatahana. 2011.

Immortelle and Bhandaaraa Poems, by Lelawattee Manoo-Rahming. 2011.

In Vitro, by Laura Solomon. 2nd ed. 2013.

Lifelines, by Shahilla Shariff. 2011.

Moving House and other Poems from Hong Kong, by Gillian Bickley. 2005.

Of Symbols Misused, by Mary-Jane Newton. 2011.

Painting the Borrowed House: Poems, by Kate Rogers. 2008.

Perceptions, by Gillian Bickley. 2012.

Rain on the Pacific Coast, by Elbert Siu Ping Lee. 2013.

refrain, by Jason S Polley. 2010.

Shadow Play, by James Norcliffe. 2012.

Shadows in Deferment, by Birgit Bunzel Linder. 2013.

Sightings: a collection of poetry, with an essay, 'communicating poems', by Gillian Bickley. 2007.

Smoked Pearl: Poems of Hong Kong and Beyond, by Akin Jeje (Akinsola Olufemi Jeje). 2010.

Unlocking, by Mary-Jane Newton. 2013.

Wonder, Lust & Itchy Feet, by Sally Dellow. 2011.

OTHER GENRES

We also publish in other genres, including fiction (novels, short story collections and novellas), autobiography, biography, children's illustrated books, educational books, Hong Kong educational and legal history, memoirs, poetry, teenage / young adult books, and travel. Other genres may be added.

FIND OUT MORE ABOUT OUR AUTHORS AND BOOKS

Visit our website: <http://www.proversepublishing.com>
Visit our distributor's website:
<www.chineseupress.com>

Follow us on Twitter
Follow news and conversation: twitter.com/Proversebooks>
OR
Copy and paste the following to your browser window and follow the instructions:
https://twitter.com/#!/ProverseBooks

Request our free E-Newsletter
Send your request to info@proversepublishing.com.

Availability
Most titles are available in Hong Kong and world-wide from our Hong Kong based Distributor,
The Chinese University Press of Hong Kong,
The Chinese University of Hong Kong, Shatin, NT,
Hong Kong SAR, China.
Email: cup-bus@cuhk.edu.hk
Website: <www.chineseupress.com>.

All titles are available from Proverse Hong Kong and the Proverse Hong Kong UK-based Distributor.

We have stock-holding retailers in Hong Kong,
Singapore (Select Books),
Canada (Elizabeth Campbell Books),
Andorra (Llibreria La Puça, La Llibreria).
Orders can be made from bookshops in the UK and elsewhere.

Ebooks
Most of our titles are available also as Ebooks.

www.ingramcontent.com/pod-product-compliance
Lightning Source LLC
Chambersburg PA
CBHW051130160426
43195CB00014B/2417